Little Skill Seekers

MAZES

■ SCHOLASTIC

New York • Toronto • London • Auckland • Sydney • New Delhi
Mexico City • Hong Kong • Buenos Aires

Cover Design: Tannaz Fassihi
Cover Illustration: Michael Robertson
Interior Design: Mina Chen
Interior Illustration: Mike Moran

ISBN: 978-1-338-25561-4
Copyright © Scholastic Inc. All rights reserved. Printed in the U.S.A.
First printing, June 2018.

1 2 3 4 5 6 7 8 9 10   40   24 23 22 21 20 19 18

Dear Parent,

Welcome to *Little Skill Seekers: Mazes*! Hand-eye coordination and fine-motor skills are important early writing skills—this workbook will help your child develop these skills.

Help your little skill seeker build a strong foundation for learning by choosing more books in the Little Skill Seekers series. The exciting and colorful workbooks in the series are designed to set your child on the path to success. Each book targets essential skills important to your child's development.

Here are some key features of *Little Skill Seekers: Mazes* and the other workbooks in this series:

- Filled with colorful illustrations that make learning fun and playful

- Provides plenty of opportunity to practice essential skills

- Builds independence as children work through the pages on their own, at their own pace

- Comes in a perfect size that fits easily in a backpack for practice on the go

Now let's get started on this journey to help your child become a successful, lifelong learner!

—The Editors

Help the boy find his horn.

Help the seahorse get to the castle.

Help the lizard get to the cactus.

Help the monkey get to the bananas.

Help the bee find the flower.

Help the superhero save the cat.

Help the man find the camel.

Help the bear get to the beehive.

Help the balloons land on the ground.

Help the taxi get to the mall.

Help the runners get to the finish line.

Help the baby find his teddy bear.

Help the racer get to the finish line.

FINISH LINE

Help the dog find the bone.

Help the rabbit find the carrots.

Help the girl get to the trophy.

Help the girl get to her bike.

Help the pterodactyl find the T. rex.

Help the girl find her sheep.

Help the boy find the treasure chest.

Help the kids get to the dock.

Help the prairie dog get to the lizard.

27

Help the penguin find her pals.

Help the children find the zebras.

Help the bird find her chicks.

Help the mouse run up the clock.

Help the man climb to the top of the mountain.

Help the spider get to her baby.

Help the builder find his tools.

Help the ants get to the food.

Help the squirrel get to the acorns.

Help the alien get to his planet.

Help the worm get to the top of the apple.

Help the Dalmatian find the firefighter.

Help each little pig get to the brick house.

Help the hamster find its friend.

Help the parrot get to the birdseed.